YOUR KNOWLEDGE HAS VALUE

- We will publish your bachelor's and master's thesis, essays and papers

- Your own eBook and book - sold worldwide in all relevant shops

- Earn money with each sale

Upload your text at www.GRIN.com and publish for free

Bibliographic information published by the German National Library:

The German National Library lists this publication in the National Bibliography; detailed bibliographic data are available on the Internet at http://dnb.dnb.de .

Imprint:

Copyright © 2015 GRIN Verlag, Open Publishing GmbH
Print and binding: Books on Demand GmbH, Norderstedt Germany
ISBN: 9783668296732

This book at GRIN:

http://www.grin.com/en/e-book/339824/developing-an-integrated-digital-marketing-plan

Ulkar Suleymanova

Developing an integrated digital marketing plan

Azerbaijan Airlines

GRIN Publishing

GRIN - Your knowledge has value

Since its foundation in 1998, GRIN has specialized in publishing academic texts by students, college teachers and other academics as e-book and printed book. The website www.grin.com is an ideal platform for presenting term papers, final papers, scientific essays, dissertations and specialist books.

Visit us on the internet:

http://www.grin.com/

http://www.facebook.com/grincom

http://www.twitter.com/grin_com

Integrated Digital Marketing Plan

Unit: E-Business & Internet Marketing

Company: Azerbaijan Airlines

This text was written by a non-native English speaker. Please excuse any errors or inconsistencies.

Executive Summary

While creating digital marketing plan for Azerbaijan Airlines (AZAL), our digital campaign`s main goal is to build better performance through digital marketing channels. The situation analysis has been held and we came to the conclusion that our campaign should follow the digital changes in the world market and fitting in the digital marketing strategies in order to reach our targeted audience.

The digital marketing plan covers the channels as above mentioned by using digital media for establishing better performance to communicate with potential customers.

We concluded that our campaign should use the following elements in order to establish better performance in digital media within communication between our customers: Web user experience, mobile presence, search marketing, search engine optimization, social media presence, activities in social networks, customer review and ratings and developing user experience within digital tools.

We have used Dave Chaffey`s "Race Method" (2010) and his great team "Smart Insights" to implement our digital marketing plan in order to reach, act, convert and engage customers within the lifecycle.

In order to develop better digital strategy, the various tools of performance proportions will be used, all actions that done based on digital marketing plan will be estimated if something would happen wrong we will develop it in early time.

Table of Contents

1. Introduction

We are going to develop our digital marketing plan within Azerbaijan National Airlines (AZAL) for reaching to the targeted audience by using right tools in the right time. As our major services are flights and online booking, we began analyzing the present situation about Airline companies, its trends and digital innovations about traveling.

The main purpose of our individual assignment is to establish digital marketing strategy about Azerbaijan Airlines (AZAL). We will start with the situation analysis, goals and objectives, marketing strategy and tactics, target audience, search marketing, ads and social network based on digital marketing plan. Our plan has focused on promoting the company and its products in order to reach to its target audience.

Azerbaijan Airlines that we are going to promote through digital marketing plan has been founded on 7th of April, 1992 and is one of the fastest growing airlines and being most powerful among the competitors in the world. Azerbaijan Airlines has focused on expanding its destinations since 1994. Being on top list, AZAL is becoming one of the key brand companies for its high service quality, flight safety and durability. Its main base is Heydar Aliyev International Airport (www.azal.az).

The main goal of our Azerbaijan Airlines is to become a local leader and well-known global airline due to its high service quality, safety and reliability. As one of the quickest developing airlines in the world, AZAL holds strategic position between East and West and strategically extends its network into Turkey, Russia, United Arab Emirates, America and Europe.

We will use the "RACE" method improved by Dave Chaffey (2010) and his great team at "Smart Insights" which is advised by professionals as a helpful and beneficial method that meets all requirements of strategic plan within building up objectives based on situation analysis in order to reach, act, convert and engage our customers throughout the lifecycle.

Using online activities, we are going to apply offline activities to analyze the digital plan that covers the "integrated" part of plan.

2. Literature Review

In recent days, digital media have become a specific part of public and private life. Young generations use digital channels in their daily lives in order to communicate, to get information and to deliver their messages within digital media. Digital media was used as a term "digital marketing" in 1990s and has grown in many countries due to its reputation in order to reach to its target audience.

According to Mulhern, Frank (2009), "digital media causes an endless growth of content, consumer networking, user-generated content and an extension of media from news and entertainment regarding with technology that has a digital interface with people".

Digital media (Internet, mobile phones and other mobile devices; digital newspapers and magazines within the Internet; digital radio and digital TV) plays an important role in our routine life.

As Rakić, Beba and Rakić, Mira notes (2014), as a result of growth of the digital media, consumers change their actions and behaviors, so that they reorient from traditional (classic) media to digital media.

As Koh, Kyungwon (2013) stated, recent research on young people's use of technology and digital media in the associated fields like education, media studies, and literacy studies, provide comprehension on youth's behaviors and features that may impress their interface with information. The main body of research explores how digital media influence to young people's lives and how digital technologies are changing the way young people study, perform, socialize, and take part in civic life.

Today Internet and digital media is growing rapidly and many people use Internet in order to book online tickets by choosing airlines. Internet, being the main part of digital media, helps customers to attract, act, convert and reach to their target audience. Digital media plays seductive role to propose on reaching buyers, getting their confidence, ensuring eventual buyer gratification in order to indicate the position of travel agency in the society.

As Chaffey and Smith notes (2008), the major benefits of digital media are as follows:

- Identifying – the Internet can be used to investigate and learn customers' needs, requirements, desires and wants
- Anticipating – Internet is an additional channel by which information can be accessed and purchases can be made

5

- Satisfying – attaining customer satisfaction within the electronic channel is the main factor in digital media

3. Situation Analysis

After the breakdown of Soviet Union, we began to build our first own airline in 1992, in Azerbaijan Airline`s Market and started to expand our destinations on November, 1994. Our first destinations were numerous key cities such as Dubai, Istanbul, Tehran, Tel-Aviv, London and St. Petersburg. It was indicated within the map in our website. In 2008, we have kept our position rated as one of the quickest growing airlines in terms of size and traffic growth.

We are one of the leading companies in Azerbaijan`s airline market with our own airplanes and in 2006 we began to propose our online flight bookings from www.azal.az and expedia.com.

- "Expedia", within company customers can learn about their flights, online-check in and baggage info and it has precisely the same online booking system as being in www.azal.az.

We are planning to open new flights to South America and North-East Asia countries and we suggest charter flights to Europe, CIS (The Commonwealth of Independent States), Middle East and Asia countries.

Strengths

- Big player in a growth market
- Strong geographic location
- Customer loyalty
- High control system
- Strong management
- Brand name

Weaknesses

- Competitive market

As our competition is very high, our brand awareness is falling.

- Bad communication

3.1 Internet Penetration in Azerbaijan

In the Soviet period, Azerbaijan was one of the main centers for Information Technology development. Internet has grown in many countries, especially in Azerbaijan. Common Internet Penetration in Azerbaijan is increasing with the help of government`s ICT strategy and Azerbaijani Diaspora for whom Internet was significant channel for providing communication with their motherland.

According to recent research, using Internet by young generations has reached to 44 percent for the latest few years.

The number of Internet users in Azerbaijan is growing per annum and today our country holds 63rd place in the world according to the report of International Telecommunication Union.

In according with the report by the Communications and High Technologies Ministry of Azerbaijan due to internet connection in 2014, 70 percent of Azerbaijan people are Internet users, 50 percent of population are broadband internet users. (www.azernews.az)

Azerbaijan has reached big success in Internet sector in the latest years. Besides, Azerbaijan stands 23th place among upcoming countries as a result of households` usage on the Internet connection.

3.2 Market Place

3.2.1 Competitors

Since Azerbaijan Airlines has started to operate for 23 years, most of companies have varied their business model for matching new market circumstances and social variations. In this case, majority of companies accepted their marketing strategy and began to propose their services online due to advantage of digital media.

According to our research, using communication channels will help companies to improve and develop based on digital marketing plan. Competitors of Azerbaijan Airlines are as follows:

- Turkish Airlines

- Aeroflot
- Lufthansa

Turkish Airlines

Turkish Airlines is the largest leading airline operating since 1933 within flights in Turkey and the best national flag carrier airline. The company has broadened its destinations to Europe and due to the number of destinations the airline has been the fourth-biggest carrier in the world. The airline operates planned services to 41 internal and 206 international airports in Europe, Asia, Africa and America.

Their website is well-organized and covers a booking form for making online flight reservation within the different forms of payment process, for making hotel reservations, car rental reservations and other associated information for visitors. By the way, Turkish Airlines is our major competitor and doing their job well. They are one of the leading European airline companies for their flight security, trustworthiness, rivalry and product, service quality.

Strengths

Their activities in Social Media like Facebook and YouTube have arranged well and propose a vast sphere of services containing "Car rental reservations" and "Award tickets with Miles/Smiles".

Weaknesses

It is difficult to build estimable staff because of expenses and high staff revolution can be hurt Turkish Airlines` power to rival.

Poor acquisition may hurt Turkish Airlines by growing their expenses and decreasing the value of their joint businesses.

A lack of distribution indicates Turkish airlines' cost per unit of outcome is very high. Rising volume, while contain quality, would assist decreasing such expenses.

Aeroflot

Aeroflot (Russian Airlines) is one of the largest airline companies in the Russian Federation and is the largest flag carrier. The airline operates internal and international passenger services.

Aeroflot is one of the oldest airlines since 1923 and under the Soviet era, the airline was the Soviet national airline and the widest airline in the world.

Their website put forward special offers (discount coupon, new comfort class) and suggest Aeroflot Bonus.

Strengths
- High development rate
- Qualified business components
- Skillful workforce
- Local market

Weaknesses
- Future rivalry
- Prices
- High credit rates

Lufthansa

Lufthansa (German Airlines) is one of the largest airline companies in Europe. Airline has broadened to 18 local destinations and 197 international destinations in 78 countries through Africa, the Americas, Asia, and Europe. German Airlines have built powerful position in the market and is one of the biggest worldwide travel companies. Lufthansa is conveyed 103 million passengers and considered one of the widest passenger airline fleets in the world.

Their website is widely growing within more detailed information. Use social media as Facebook and YouTube, the airline has Facebook page consisting of 1,815,883 likes.

Strengths

- IT segmentation
- Rent of planes
- Widest Star Alliance Member
- Global actions

Weaknesses

- Growth rate of low price
- Biggest Star Alliance Member

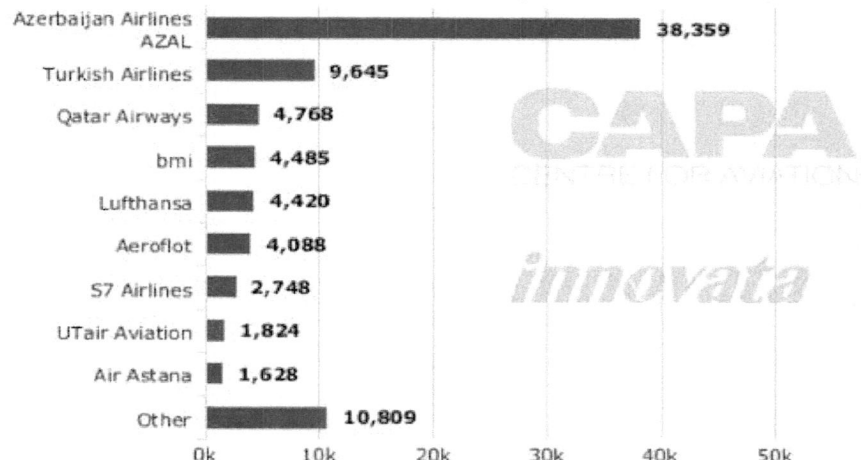

Figure 1. Baku Heydar Aliyev International Airport international capacity by carrier (seats per week). Source: CAPA – Centre for Aviation & Innovata

3.2.2 KSF and USP of Azerbaijan Airlines

	KSF and USP of Azerbaijan Airlines
KSF	Well-organized, effective sales force, superior information systems and brand reputation.
USP	Azerbaijan Airlines offers their customers to earn certain bonuses and benefits. Within "AZAL MILES" program, the customers can earn the number of points.

3.3 Online audience and customer analysis

As our targeted audiences are vacationers, business travelers, couples, students and families who are traveling to/from Azerbaijan and the countries they prefer are basically Turkey, Russia and European countries. The digital marketing plan that we are going to implement will be focused on the same audience and market segmentation too. The digital marketing plan will cover the people who are ages of 18-65 years old that which our market is segmented.

Our targeted audiences are mainly students who use Internet in their daily lives and majority of them are online ticket buyers of Azerbaijan Hava Yollari Airlines (AZAL). As well, they are permanent users of Social media and YouTube. The website and social media play an important role for reaching more detailed information to their online audiences.
We use social media to reach our targeted audience, to enhance branding awareness between customers and to carry out digital marketing techniques based on digital marketing plan. "Social media is an interactive media" (Mayfield, 2008).

Facebook

In Azerbaijan, in accordance with the annual Caucasus Barometer review (2013), 57 % of the people utilizing the Internet in order to get the information and to aware of social media`s activities. Facebook is the most famous social network in Azerbaijan and the majority of people use Facebook in their daily lives.

According to the Caucasus Barometer, 85 % of the Facebook users are young-aged people between 18-35 years old, 13% of the Facebook users are middle-aged people and 2 % of them are old-aged people. The majority of users are males (65 % regarding to the Social bakers statistics in 2014) spending their time in Facebook and 68 % in accordance with the Caucasus Barometer.

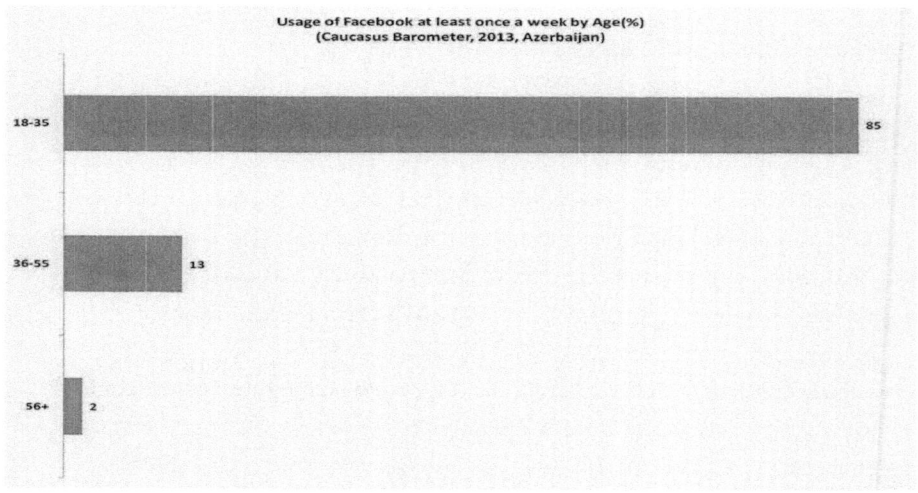

Figure 2. Usage of Facebook by age in Azerbaijan (CB, 2013)

CB indicates that Facebook is growing rapidly and very effectively for reaching to its targeted audience.

YouTube

YouTube is very useful video social network which utilized by Azerbaijanis and the majority of the young people use it for reaching its targeted audience. We are going to promote our company`s videos within YouTube in order to attract and engage people.

Regarding to the statistical center Global Stats, the number of users in YouTube has grown fast in Azerbaijan.

Usage of Social media has widely disseminated in Turkey, Russia and European countries where our targeted audience are traveling frequently.

Turkey – According to Wikipedia, Turkey has 35 million active Internet users. Most of the people using Facebook, Twitter and Google+ and regarding to the Figure 3, Instagram is less used by the people who are permanent Internet users in Turkey.

Russia – In accordance with the Wikipedia, Internet in Russia had grown since 1991 and spread to the world within EUnet (European UNIX Network). It was available to access to Internet by home users, business men through dial-up, cable, Wi-Fi (wireless connection) and mobile. In 2011, due to the peak number of Internet users and online visitors, Russia exceeded Germany in the European market. In 2013, Russia was one of the second largest used languages in the web. Internet users in Russia are mainly young people, who spend more time using VKontakte, Facebook and Odnoklassniki. But less people are using Google+ and Twitter.

European Countries – Internet in the European countries has increased rapidly and 90 % of the population is online users. According to the Figure 5, Iceland and Norway are the leading countries using Internet frequently and they are on the top list.

3.4 Current & Past Online Presence

We have to mention that our digital campaign was operating from 1992 and first of all, we created our official website and shared our digital information within Social media (Facebook, Twitter, YouTube and Instagram). We added more videos through YouTube video social

13

network in order to promote our campaign, to increase brand awareness and get information about past and current online presence of our campaign. If we told about past online presence of our campaign, we should also mention the current online presence of our digital campaign. The website and Social Media hold an important place in the development of our campaign. We should make a note that our campaign is growing rapidly through our official website, Social Media, YouTube and other online communication channels.

3.4.1 Website User Experience and Mobile presence

Our official website is well-organized and it has very creative, colorful design which is engaging customers to visit our campaign's website. On the web, usability is a necessary condition for survival (Nielsen, 2003).

The users can read website in three languages which they prefer (native-Azerbaijan, Russian, English), and while joining to website, the users can make hotel and flight reservations from booking. They may check-in their flight details and timetable from check-in. If new user visits website first time, Search Engines will help to her/him to find more information about flight details, online bookings. Its full page contains detailed information about special offers and awards of our campaign. In the top of the page, you can see our campaign's offers and can get much more information. In the right side, our campaign offers our customers to earn certain bonuses and benefits. While we are traveling abroad with Azerbaijan Airlines (AZAL), each flight which is counted by the number of points depending on the distance of our trip will be added to our personal account. When we are going to buy ticket from AZAL, we should present our card approving our presence in the "AZAL MILES" program to ticket sales agent. Earning the number of points we will gain the following bonuses:

- Free baggage benefits
- Free updates from economy to business
- Free tickets by Azerbaijan airlines

If users want to get information about flight dates within mobile applications (Android, IPhone and etc.) they can download Baku Airport app for more information and this app informs when airplanes are landing on and taking off. We are developing through mobile app in order to reach our targeted audience. Within mobile, users can access to website and make online flight booking from Azerbaijan Airlines.

3.4.2 Social Media Presence

According to Loop and Malyshev (2013), "social media presence can demonstrate itself in a variety of ways—from commenting on websites and social media platforms like Twitter, LinkedIn, Facebook and beyond—but in all instances, it designs the company's brand to untold numbers of people".

Our campaign is developing within Social Media activities such as Facebook, YouTube and etc. If we are going to look our campaign's Facebook page, we will see how many likers, followers and comments does our campaign have? Our campaign's Facebook page has reached to 15,614 likes and only 119 people talking about this. Our Facebook page will help customers to get more information about flight details and engage, attract customers for buying online tickets.

We will promote our digital campaign using YouTube videos. It will help customers on getting information about our airlines campaign, its safety and benefits.

3.4.3 Search Marketing Presence

Search Engines are an unusual possibility to promote our campaign's services and products in time when customers are searching from Google or other engines. Google is one the largest search engines in the world. When we are going to search our campaign from Google, we find 735, 000 results about Azerbaijan Hava Yollari Airlines (AZAL).

4. Plan of action

We are going to implement an action plan using inbound marketing in order to meet our campaign's requirements.

According to Winterberg, Bill (2013), "Inbound marketing is the practice of making your campaign easy to find, and drawing potential clients to your website and other media through content they find valuable and personally relevant".

An action plan contains a number of action steps based on digital marketing plan. Today web presence is very significant for promoting the campaign and within inbound marketing our

15

airlines campaign will be developed. Inbound Marketing will be our major communication channel.

4.1 Objectives

We are going to build objectives based on digital marketing plan. The main objectives of our airlines are as follows:

- Becoming most preferred carrier on the international flights
- Connecting other major cities in Europe and Asia among Azerbaijan
- Enhancing annual income from flights for holding financial status high
- Assist to upcoming growth of our campaign
- Secure of our campaign's products in the world aircraft market

4.2 Targeting and Segmentation

As our target audiences are vacationers, business travelers, couples, students and families who are traveling to/from Azerbaijan to the following countries: Turkey, Russia and European countries.

Our targeted audience will be students, families and business people who are traveling from/to Azerbaijan. We are going to build peculiar segmented campaigns for reaching international purchasers who wish to travel from/to Azerbaijan.
Our segments include:

- **Students** – who are going to study abroad by sending from the universities within the projects and during staying long term and short term, traveling all over the world
- **Families** – who are traveling during holidays, summer and vacations
- **Business people** – who are going to do business and make shopping.

We are going to do special offers for customers with inexpensive prices in order to book their flights easier and quicker. We will exceed our competitors and its great offer for our targeted audience.

Our campaign`s key message is:

Azerbaijan

"Azərbaycan Hava Yollarının" ən vacib vəzifəsi uçuşların təhlükəsizliyinin təminatıdır"

English

"Flight safety is a top priority for Azerbaijan Airlines"

4.3 Reach

We are going to utilize numerous digital channels in order to reach to our targeted audience and going to gain advantages from the weaknesses of our competitors.

4.3.1 Search Marketing

If we are going to website and don't see any search results, what are we going to do? Are we looking for search engines through social sites? Yes, we are going to find something through social sites, but we should consider our website`s place in Search engines.

As Panda, Tapan K. note (2013), Search Marketing is a type of Internet Marketing that promotes websites in order to enhance the visibility within SEO.
Search Marketing is an efficient method in order to reach to our potential customers. Therefore, we will make it using paid, unpaid search marketing procedures and Search Engine optimization.

We will build CPC campaigns as the major goal of our campaigns is to enhance annual incomes from online bookings for use-action which is needed in search marketing. Therefore we are going to pay just for users` clicks who will find our campaign according to search engines.

Keyword	Avg. Monthly Searches	Competition	Suggested bid	Impr. share	In account?	In plan?
azal airlines	1600	0.15	0.15	--	N	N
azal azerbaijan airlines	30	0.17	0.24	--	N	N
azal airline	50	0.15	0.24	--	N	N
azal airlines online booking	20	0.43	0.12	--	N	N
azal airlines timetable	10	0.15	0.28	--	N	N
azal airlines uk	10	0.34		--	N	N
azal	14800	0.06	0.11	--	N	N
azal air	140	0.15	0.09	--	N	N
azal flights	30	0.25	0.02	--	N	N
azal check in	30	0.05	0.17	--	N	N
azal airways	20	0.14		--	N	N
azal online ticket	20	0.35	0.02	--	N	N
azal web check in	10	0		--	N	N
azal flight	10	0.07		--	N	N
azal flight timetable	10	0.23		--	N	N
baku istanbul flights	40	0.4	0.43	--	N	N
flights from baku	30	0.13	0.6	--	N	N

Figure 3. Designing of Search Marketing keywords from Google Keyword Planner

Google Adwords

We are going to build keywords for our campaign and key pointers for our Google Adwords campaign are: number of clicks, Cost per click and number of bookings.

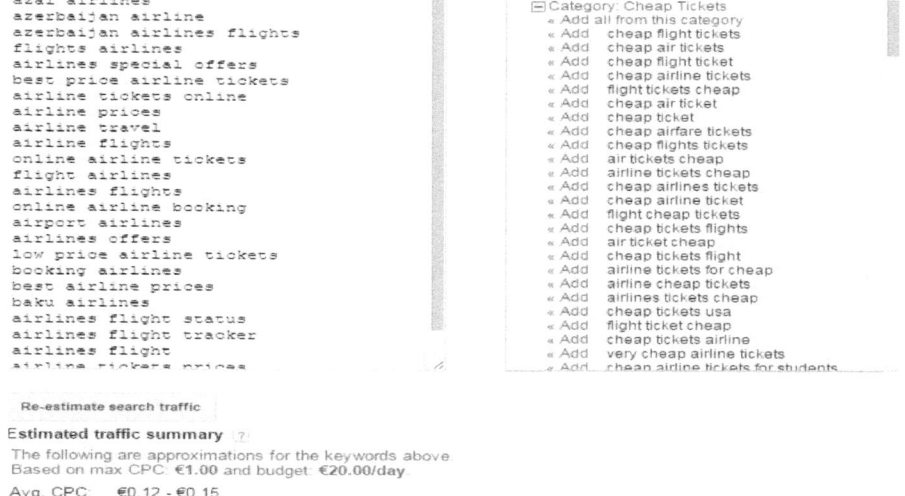

Figure 4. Ad on Google Adwords

18

As we have shown above, the average of CPC is not very high even though they contain other powerful keywords.

Search Engine Optimization

According to Harrigan, Paul and Hulbert, Bev (2011), "SEO (search engine optimization) is a driver of new marketing approaches".
We will use both types of SEO, on-site and off-site optimization. KPI (Key Performance Indicator) of our campaign are: visits, period staying on site, inbound and outbound connections, Google Page rating and SEO Grade.

On-site Optimization

- Developing the web`s performance (color, structure, design and size)
- Increasing the web`s quality in high level
- Make it attractive to engage customers
- Growing rank system and visibility

Off-site optimization
- Improving web`s content through videos and blogs
- Building articles for customers to publish it in webpages and blogs

4.3.2 Facebook pay per click (PPC) ads

We have built the Facebook ads for our campaign in order to reach our targeted audience. The Key performance indicator of our campaign will be: fans, followers, subscribers, comments and likes. Our targeted audience has been defined as follows:

CAMPAIGN   **BUDGET and PRICING**

We have created Facebook page in order to promote our campaign and engage customers to visit our official Facebook page.

4.4 Act & Convert

4.4.1 Website optimization & User Experience

We are going to design again our whole website in a different way in order to meet our customers' wants, needs and requirements. We will have the key elements of the website as follows:

- User experience – more detailed information and ease of use
- Optimized – optimized for search creepers
- Attention – to assure that first read will be special suggestions, second will be online booking and last will be support
- Sharing videos – it will help customers to find our product very easy
- Integration of social networks – we suggest to integrate the major social networks (Facebook, Instagram and Twitter) in each page of the website which it will be visible for everyone

KPI – booking, reviews and support tickets

We can follow the performance of our website through **Google Analytics** and **AddThis.com**.

4.5 Engage

4.5.1 Customer service and support

We will start to use Live Chat support to communicate with our customers at any time and our main goal is to help our customers if they have difficulties to find any information about our campaign. When log in to Live Chat, all activities will be saved, tested and evaluated from our campaign agents to ensure the highest quality in customer support.

4.5.2 Reviews and Ratings

Engaging customer cooperation through product review and ratings appends to the productivity of the content too. The reviews will be indicated in the booking process which is implemented by our campaign.

5. Conclusion

The digital marketing plan we have implemented will help on reaching our whole objectives within the activities of Social Media. The all actions done in this plan will be checked and estimated during the implementation of digital marketing plan.

After finishing it, we used various KPI`s for each tactic and the tactic that we used is very pliable and quantifiable. The most important fact is that if anything will not work, we can instantly achieve with it.

Regarding with the plan, the screen of user`s indicators and performance tools will be used in accordance with Social Bakers, Caucasus Barometer and Google Analytics.

Based on the research we are going to come to a decision what strategy we should use, which tactics, which channels we will use and what kind of things attracting customers` attention thus we can develop our campaign more efficient.

6. Bibliography

Chaffey, D. and Smith, P.R. (2008) *eMarketing eXcellence: Planning and Optimizing Your Digital Marketing, 3rd Edition*, Oxford, UK: Butterworth Heinemann Publishing

Chaffey, D. and Smith, P.R. (2013) *eMarketing eXcellence: Planning and Optimizing Your Digital Marketing, 4th Edition*, p. 292. Oxford, UK: Butterworth Heinemann Publishing

Harrigan, Paul, and Bev Hulbert (2011) How Can Marketing Academics Serve Marketing Practice? The New Marketing DNA as a Model for Marketing Education. *Journal of Marketing Education,* 33 (3), 253, 272.
Available from: http://web.b.ebscohost.com/ehost/detail/detail?vid=16&sid=76f036d1-5ad4-4f89-9915-2834aed7f3c0%40sessionmgr113&hid=101&bdata=JnNpdGU9ZWhvc3QtbGl2ZQ%3d%3d#db=bth&AN=67716109 [Accessed 1st December, 2011].

Koh, Kyungwon (2013) Adolescents' Information-Creating Behavior Embedded in Digital Media Practice Using Scratch. *Journal of the American Society for Information Science & Technology*, 64 (9), 1826, 1841.
Available from: http://web.a.ebscohost.com/ehost/pdfviewer/pdfviewer?sid=998d11aa-a9f2-4221-85f7-9f928ab60a27%40sessionmgr4001&vid=22&hid=4109 [Accessed 1st September, 2013].

Loop, Jeffrey L. and Malyshev, Alexander G. (2013) How to Manage a Company's Social Media Presence. *Intellectual Property & Technology Law Journal*, 25 (4), 3, 8. Available from: http://web.a.ebscohost.com/ehost/pdfviewer/pdfviewer?sid=d8abb7b6-9e51-4860-a0b5-b31ce39e931c%40sessionmgr4003&vid=12&hid=4206 [Accessed 1st April, 2013].

Mulhern, Frank. (2009) Integrated marketing communications: From media channels to digital connectivity. *Journal of Marketing Communications*, 15 (2), 85, 101. Available from: http://web.a.ebscohost.com/ehost/pdfviewer/pdfviewer?vid=14&sid=998d11aa-a9f2-4221-85f7-9f928ab60a27%40sessionmgr4001&hid=4109 [Accessed 1st April, 2009].

Mayfield, A. (2008) *What is social media?* An e-book from Icrossing. Available from: www.icrossing.co.uk

Panda, Tapan K (2013) Search Engine Marketing: Does the Knowledge Discovery Process Help Online Retailers? *IUP Journal of Knowledge Management*, 11 (3), 55, 66. Available from: http://web.b.ebscohost.com/ehost/pdfviewer/pdfviewer?vid=31&sid=76f036d1-5ad4-4f89-9915-2834aed7f3c0%40sessionmgr113&hid=101 [Accessed 1st July, 2013].

Rakić, Beba and Rakić, Mira (2014) Integrated Marketing Communications Paradigm in Digital Environment: The Five Pillars of Integration. *Megatrend Review*, 11 (1), 187, 203. Available   from: http://web.b.ebscohost.com/ehost/pdfviewer/pdfviewer?vid=6&sid=76f036d1-5ad4-4f89-9915-2834aed7f3c0%40sessionmgr113&hid=101[Accessed 1st January, 2014].

Winterberg, Bill (2013) Tools for Digital Age Marketing. *Journal of Financial Planning*, 26(1), 32, 33. Available from: http://web.b.ebscohost.com/ehost/pdfviewer/pdfviewer?sid=9f115eff-6f41-487f-b30f-a03d7dc8e50a%40sessionmgr112&vid=37&hid=109 [Accessed 1st January, 2013].

Wikipedia (2012) Internet in Azerbaijan. (Online)
Available from: http://en.wikipedia.org/wiki/Internet_in_Azerbaijan [Accessed 02/01/15].

Wikipedia (2012) Internet in Russia. (Online)
Available from: http://en.wikipedia.org/wiki/Internet_in_Russia [Accessed 21/11/14].

Wikipedia (2012) Internet in Turkey. (Online)
Available from: http://en.wikipedia.org/wiki/Internet_in_Turkey [Accessed 12/12/14].

7. Appendices

Sources
Azerbaijan Airlines

www.azal.az
https://www.facebook.com/www.azal.az
http://www.azernews.az/business/69225.html
http://www.today.az/news/society/136797.html

https://www.google.az/url?sa=i&rct=j&q=&esrc=s&source=images&cd=&cad=rja&uact=8&
ved=0CAcQjRw&url=http%3A%2F%2Fcentreforaviation.com%2Fanalysis%2Fazerbaijan-
airlines-expands-network-as-azerbaijan-aims-to-raise-tourism-profile-
75963&ei=5NOrVJDkOpPbaMeHgMgG&psig=AFQjCNHvsOurHiSVi-
ya3gmOeafc3TKGYg&ust=1420633349691159

Turkish Airlines
http://www.turkishairlines.com/en-int/

Russian Airlines
https://www.aeroflot.ru/cms/en/

German Airlines
http://www.lufthansa.com/online/portal/lh/gr/homepage

Figure Sources
http://crrc-caucasus.blogspot.gr/2014/07/facebook-usage-in-azerbaijan.html
http://www.mincom.gov.az/media-en/news-2/details/8110
http://www.statista.com
http://wearesocial.net/blog/2014/02/social-digital-mobile-europe-2014/

YOUR KNOWLEDGE HAS VALUE

- We will publish your bachelor's and
  master's thesis, essays and papers

- Your own eBook and book -
  sold worldwide in all relevant shops

- Earn money with each sale

Upload your text at www.GRIN.com
and publish for free